WELCOME TO THE CHURCH OF THE NAZARENE

THE FOUNDRY
PUBLISHING

Copyright © 2019 by The Foundry Publishing
The Foundry Publishing
PO Box 419527
Kansas City, MO 64141
thefoundrypublishing.com

ISBN 978-0-8341-3825-4

Printed in the
United States of America

Cover design: Arthur Cherry
Interior design: Sharon Page

Library of Congress Cataloging-in-Publication Data
A complete catalog record for this book is available from the Library of Congress.

All Scripture quotations, unless otherwise indicated, are from the Holy Bible, New International Version® (NIV®). Copyright © 1973, 1978, 1984, 2011 by Biblica, Inc.™ Used by permission of Zondervan. All rights reserved worldwide. www.zondervan.com. The "NIV" and "New International Version" are trademarks registered in the United States Patent and Trademark Office by Biblica, Inc.™

The internet addresses, email addresses, and phone numbers in this book are accurate at the time of publication. They are provided as a resource. The Foundry Publishing does not endorse them or vouch for their content or permanence.

10 9 8 7 6 5 4 3 2 1

CONTENTS

I. INTRODUCTION
ONE
CHURCH
AMONG
MANY

Have you ever moved to a new place—maybe a small town or perhaps a large city—and tried to look for a church to attend? Where will you and your family feel accepted? How will you find a church that feels like a good fit for you? And if you do find a church that feels right, what does that church believe and support? How is it different from all of the other churches in town?

Sometimes it's hard to find a new church that feels like home. If you're single, you may worry about fitting in and finding your place. If you have children, you may wonder if your kids will be accepted in their new environment. If you are busy raising adolescents and teens, you may be searching for a church that features high-quality youth ministry while also providing a full calendar of safe and fun activities that your teens will enjoy.

Finding a new church isn't easy, whether you've moved across the country or you're just trying to make a new start. Hopefully this little book can help you understand one of your many options: your local Nazarene church.

If you haven't heard of any Nazarene churches before, don't worry. Although the global Church of the Nazarene has almost three million members, it's a lot smaller than other denominations such as the Southern Baptists and the Roman Catholics—both of whom have many millions more in attendance all around the world. If you've heard of Methodists or Wesleyans, you'll discover that Nazarenes are part of that same branch of the Christian family. We'll explore that connection later in this book.

Meanwhile, if you live near a Nazarene university, you may already be familiar with the Church of the Nazarene. For instance, many people in and around the San Diego area are familiar with the Nazarene denomination because of Point Loma Nazarene University. Parents send their students to Point Loma even if they don't have a religious affiliation or Christian background because they know the university will provide a high-quality education. Nazarenes have always made higher education a priority. From Olivet Nazarene University near Chicago to Eastern Nazarene College near Boston, there are many people who know the word "Nazarene" because of an excellent school nearby.

As we begin to explore your decision to attend a Nazarene church, let's look at where the Church of the Nazarene fits within the larger scope of Christianity and Christian faith. To do that, in the next chapter we'll examine how Christian history leads up to today's global Church of the Nazarene. From the first century to the twenty-first, Christians have expressed their faith in many ways. As we shall see, the Church of the Nazarene has also contributed its own unique expression to the Christian story.

2. HISTORY
WHERE WE
COME FROM

The Christian church began in the first century, following the crucifixion, resurrection, and ascension of Jesus. It became a reality at the outpouring of the Holy Spirit on the day of Pentecost. Within three hundred years, Christianity was the most powerful force in the Roman world, becoming in the fourth century the official religion of the empire. The church encompassed what became the Eastern Orthodox Church and the Roman Catholic Church.

During the Middle Ages, several reform movements developed in the Roman Catholic Church, and in the sixteenth century, the Protestant Reformation, led by Martin Luther and others, gave birth to many of the great denominations we know today.

In the early eighteenth century, the evangelical revival in England began, nurtured chiefly by the ministry of Anglican clerics John Wesley, Charles Wesley, and George Whitefield. Their emphasis was upon living a victorious life through the indwelling presence of the Holy Spirit. Especially notable was John Wesley, who encouraged Christians to gather in small groups for transparent, accountable Bible study and prayer. This "method" for helping Christians grow in their faith is where the name "Methodist" comes from. Today's Methodist denominations arose from following John Wesley's ideas on personal growth and holiness.

As the years passed, the preaching and teaching of the doctrine of the Spirit-filled life, sometimes called entire sanctification or Christian holiness, began to wane. In North America, this resulted in the organization of such denominations as the Wesleyan Methodist and Free Methodist Churches, which sought to revive the doctrinal emphases of John Wesley.

In the latter part the nineteenth century, Methodists and many other Protestants experienced a widespread holiness revival. Out of this revival many "holiness associations" were formed in North America. But the movement was by no means popular, and opposition to the message arose. This forced these groups to band together in loose organizations for mutual encouragement and support. It was out of this movement that the Church of the Nazarene was born. A partial survey of the groups that formed the Church of the Nazarene would include the following:

New England

A congregation in Providence, Rhode Island, found that it had much in common with a separate congregation in Boston, Massachusetts. As the two pastors and their congregations began to talk, other like-minded churches joined the conversation. The result was a union of ten congregations that took place on March 13-14, 1890, in the village of Rock, Massachusetts. In spiritual focus and theological thought, this union of ten churches is a precursor to today's Nazarene congregations.

New York

In 1894, a businessman in Brooklyn, New York, wanted to help spread the idea of becoming more holy, more loving, and more godly. He organized an independent church with thirty-two members, then two other churches. Similar churches were also started in adjacent states. They learned about the New England congregations. As a result, the New England and Mid-Atlantic groups joined together. The union of like-minded churches was growing, and two congregations were organized in Canada in 1902. By 1907, this eastern group stretched from Nova Scotia to Iowa.

Tennessee

Also in 1894, a church was formed in Milan, Tennessee, led by evangelist R. L. Harris. The new congregation was theologically similar to the New England churches. Its influence quickly spread from Tennessee to Arkansas and West Texas.

California

At exactly this same moment in history, a new congregation formed in Los Angeles based on the same ideas and beliefs that were uniting the groups back east. The people invited Rev. Phineas Bresee and Dr. J. P. Widney to be their pastors. Thus, in 1895, the first congregation was formed that was called by the name "Church of the Nazarene."

The California group—united around the principal ideas of growing and becoming holy and more like God—also featured a notable emphasis on making society and their local community better. Bresee and others reached out to alcoholics, prostitutes, and others—anyone who belonged to a people group often overlooked by churches or looked down on by religious people. Bresee insisted that the good news of Jesus Christ was always meant for "the least of these" (see Matthew 25:40), and his church was located in an area where the outcasts of society could be found. It was not uncommon for the church to meet together on Sunday for worship and then spend the balance of the day in fellowship and community life, reaching out to include and transform those who needed God the most.

Ten years later, the original Los Angeles church had become the center for a larger group of churches along the Pacific Coast, including Seattle and

Spokane, Washington, and Berkeley and Oakland, California. It had even moved east, with churches in Utah, Iowa, and Illinois, including a large church in Chicago.

Texas

In 1901, Rev. C. B. Jernigan organized the Independent Holiness Church in Van Alstyne, Texas. This group spread through eastern Texas and Oklahoma Territory. In 1904, this group met with the one that began in Tennessee. They voted to merge and organized their beliefs and practices and published them in a book called a Manual (an organizational handbook and also a statement of beliefs). By late 1908, the unified group was centered in Texas, Arkansas, and Tennessee and had congregations in Georgia and New Mexico.

At this point—the early years of the twentieth century—there were three significantly sized groups, in three different parts of the country, consisting of people who essentially believed the same things and focused on the same core ideas of Christian growth and holiness. With technology and travel making broader communication possible, the groups talked with and learned from one another.

The eastern and western groups made contact with one another and negotiated a merger, which was finalized in 1907 at the First General Assembly, held in Chicago. Observers from the southern group were present and went home to testify to the amazing sense of unity and shared purpose they had witnessed at the assembly.

They invited the new denomination to hold the Second General Assembly one year later, at Pilot Point, Texas, the southern group's denominational headquarters. The Second General Assembly made history. There, on Tuesday, October 13, 1908, the denomination now known as the Church of the Nazarene was finalized by the unanimous vote of delegates representing three geographical regions. The union of these three groups in 1907 and 1908 gave the early Church of the Nazarene its essential character.

In the early years of the twentieth century, other like-minded groups joined the growing movement. In 1915, a group of churches in the United Kingdom joined the US-based Nazarene denomination. That same year, a group in the southeastern United States also joined the new organization. Growth was rapid and ongoing. In 1922, a movement in the Dakotas known as the Layman's Holiness Association also merged with the Church of the Nazarene, bringing along its more than one thousand members. Congregations across the United States and in the British Isles were united by a common purpose and now also by a common statement of faith, a common Manual, and a shared organizational structure.

By the end of 2018, there were 30,712 local Nazarene churches spread throughout 162 world areas. There were nearly seven hundred missionaries serving to spread the good news of Christ in even more places, planting more churches, and uniting Christians around the idea of growing and maturing in Christ and becoming more holy. Today, the top leaders of the Nazarene denomination trace their own roots to Africa, Central America, and Europe, in addition to North America. The Nazarene denomination is truly a global church with a worldwide mission.

3. THEOLOGY
OUR CORE AND
BASIC BELIEFS

Nazarenes, as part of the global family of Christians, express their beliefs using a historic document of faith often known as the Apostles' Creed. Crafted and created in the first few centuries after Christ's life, death, resurrection, and ascension, this common statement of faith has been adopted and ratified by Christian believers of many denominations. It is a place of unity and agreement for scholars, theologians, pastors, students of the Bible, and the rest of us who consider ourselves to be followers of Jesus in the twenty-first century.

You may have seen this creed before. You may have read these words as part of a church service at Easter or at some other time of the year. Some denominations recite the creed in their church services regularly. Here, in plain English, is this historic expression of what it means to believe in Jesus Christ and what it means to share in the global community of faithful Christian believers.

The Apostles' Creed

I believe in God the Father Almighty,
Maker of heaven and earth;

And in Jesus Christ, His only Son, our Lord:
who was conceived by the Holy Spirit,
born of the Virgin Mary,

suffered under Pontius Pilate,
was crucified, dead, and buried;
He descended into hades;
the third day He rose again from the dead;
He ascended into heaven,
and sitteth at the right hand of God
the Father Almighty;
from thence He shall come to judge the
living and the dead.

I believe in the Holy Spirit,
the holy Church universal,
the communion of saints,
the forgiveness of sins,
the resurrection of the body,
and the life everlasting.
Amen.[1]

The Apostles' Creed forms the first building block of our statements of belief, uniting today's Church of the Nazarene with Christ's first disciples, with the earliest Christians, and with the major leaders and thinkers of Christianity. Reciting the creed establishes a historic connection with the core of Christian believers who have kept the faith, following God's Word as the standard for daily liv-

---

1. *Sing to the Lord* (Kansas City: Lillenas, 1993), no. 8.

ing since the early decades after Christ and on down through many centuries. The Apostles' Creed is not nationalistic or cultural; it is the distilled essence of Christian belief.

The Articles of Faith

Nazarenes, as part of the global family of Christians, have spent decades reflecting on their beliefs and forming a statement of faith that unites Nazarenes around the world in basic agreement on key ideas. Whether you call this type of statement a doctrine or a theology, it is a succinct statement of core beliefs, helping Nazarenes find their place among the diversity of Christian thought.

The Nazarene Articles of Faith are a work in progress, considered and often revised during the quadrennial assemblies of the global denomination (see chapter 4 on how the Church of the Nazarene is organized). Although there are changes in the language that communicate our Articles of Faith, the core ideas are resolute.

Careful to always use the Bible as a guide, Nazarene theologians and editors have placed Scripture references within each section of the Articles. These are the Articles of Faith that the Church of the Nazarene has adopted, revised, refined, and affirmed across more than a century of our history.

They are reprinted (including any revisions) every four years in each new edition of the *Church of the Nazarene Manual*. The ones printed here come from the 2017-21 edition of the *Manual*.

I. The Triune God

1. We believe in one eternally existent, infinite God, Sovereign Creator and Sustainer of the universe; that He only is God, holy in nature, attributes, and purpose. The God who is holy love and light is Triune in essential being, revealed as Father, Son, and Holy Spirit.

(Genesis 1; Leviticus 19:2; Deuteronomy 6:4-5; Isaiah 5:16; 6:1-7; 40:18-31; Matthew 3:16-17; 28:19-20; John 14:6-27; 1 Corinthians 8:6; 2 Corinthians 13:14; Galatians 4:4-6; Ephesians 2:13-18; 1 John 1:5; 4:8)

II. Jesus Christ

2. We believe in Jesus Christ, the Second Person of the Triune Godhead; that He was eternally one with the Father; that He became incarnate by the Holy Spirit and was born of the Virgin Mary, so that two whole and perfect natures, that is to say the Godhead and manhood, are thus united in one Person very God and very man, the God-man.

We believe that Jesus Christ died for our sins, and that He truly arose from the dead and took again His body, together with all things appertaining to the perfection of man's nature, wherewith He ascended into heaven and is there engaged in intercession for us.

(Matthew 1:20-25; 16:15-16; Luke 1:26-35; John 1:1-18; Acts 2:22-36; Romans 8:3, 32-34; Galatians 4:4-5; Philippians 2:5-11; Colossians 1:12-22; 1 Timothy 6:14-16; Hebrews 1:1-5; 7:22-28; 9:24-28; 1 John 1:1-3; 4:2-3, 15)

III. The Holy Spirit

3. We believe in the Holy Spirit, the Third Person of the Triune Godhead, that He is ever present and efficiently active in and with the Church of Christ, convincing the world of sin, regenerating those who repent and believe, sanctifying believers, and guiding into all truth as it is in Jesus.

(John 7:39; 14:15-18, 26; 16:7-15; Acts 2:33; 15:8-9; Romans 8:1-27; Galatians 3:1-14; 4:6; Ephesians 3:14-21; 1 Thessalonians 4:7-8; 2 Thessalonians 2:13; 1 Peter 1:2; 1 John 3:24; 4:13)

IV. The Holy Scriptures

4. We believe in the plenary inspiration of the Holy Scriptures, by which we understand the 66 books of the Old and New Testaments, given by divine inspiration, inerrantly revealing the will of God concerning us in all things necessary to our salvation, so that whatever is not contained therein is not to be enjoined as an article of faith.

(Luke 24:44-47; John 10:35; 1 Corinthians 15:3-4; 2 Timothy 3:15-17; 1 Peter 1:10-12; 2 Peter 1:20-21)

V. Sin, Original and Personal

5. We believe that sin came into the world through the disobedience of our first parents, and death by sin. We believe that sin is of two kinds: original sin or depravity, and actual or personal sin.

5.1. We believe that original sin, or depravity, is that corruption of the nature of all the offspring of Adam by reason of which everyone is very far gone from original righteousness or the pure state of our first parents at the time of their creation, is averse to God, is without spiritual life, and inclined to evil, and that continually. We further believe that original sin continues to exist with the new life of the regenerate, until the heart is fully cleansed by the baptism with the Holy Spirit.

5.2. We believe that original sin differs from actual sin in that it constitutes an inherited propensity to actual sin for which no one is accountable until its divinely provided remedy is neglected or rejected.

5.3. We believe that actual or personal sin is a voluntary violation of a known law of God by a morally responsible person. It is therefore not to be confused with involuntary and inescapable shortcomings, infirmities, faults, mistakes, failures, or other deviations from a standard of perfect conduct that are the residual effects of the Fall. However, such innocent effects do not include attitudes or responses contrary to the spirit of Christ, which may properly be called sins of the spirit. We believe that personal sin is primarily and essentially a violation of the law of love; and that in relation to Christ sin may be defined as unbelief.

(Original sin: Genesis 3; 6:5; Job 15:14; Psalm 51:5; Jeremiah 17:9-10; Mark 7:21-23; Romans 1:18-25; 5:12-14; 7:1–8:9; 1 Corinthians 3:1-4; Galatians 5:16-25; 1 John 1:7-8

Personal sin: Matthew 22:36-40 {with 1 John 3:4}; John 8:34-36; 16:8-9; Romans 3:23; 6:15-23; 8:18-24; 14:23; 1 John 1:9–2:4; 3:7-10)

VI. Atonement

6. We believe that Jesus Christ, by His sufferings, by the shedding of His own blood, and by His death on the Cross, made a full atonement for all human sin, and that this Atonement is the only ground of salvation, and that it is sufficient for every individual of Adam's race. The Atonement is graciously efficacious for the salvation of those incapable of moral responsibility and for the children in innocency but is efficacious for the salvation of those who reach the age of responsibility only when they repent and believe.

(Isaiah 53:5-6, 11; Mark 10:45; Luke 24:46-48; John 1:29; 3:14-17; Acts 4:10-12; Romans 3:21-26; 4:17-25; 5:6-21; 1 Corinthians 6:20; 2 Corinthians 5:14-21; Galatians 1:3-4; 3:13-14; Colossians 1:19-23; 1 Timothy 2:3-6; Titus 2:11-14; Hebrews 2:9; 9:11-14; 13:12; 1 Peter 1:18-21; 2:19-25; 1 John 2:1-2)

VII. Prevenient Grace

7. We believe that the grace of God through Jesus Christ is freely bestowed upon all people, enabling all who will to turn from sin to righteousness, believe on Jesus Christ for pardon and cleansing from sin, and follow good works pleasing and acceptable in His sight. We also believe that the human race's creation in Godlikeness included the ability to choose between right and wrong, and that thus human beings were made morally responsible; that through the fall of Adam they became depraved so that they cannot now turn and prepare themselves by their own natural strength and works to faith and calling upon God.

(Godlikeness and moral responsibility: Genesis 1:26-27; 2:16-17; Deuteronomy 28:1-2; 30:19; Joshua 24:15; Psalm 8:3-5; Isaiah 1:8-10; Jeremiah 31:29-30; Ezekiel 18:1-4; Micah 6:8; Romans 1:19-20; 2:1-16; 14:7-12; Galatians 6:7-8

Natural inability: Job 14:4; 15:14; Psalms 14:1-4; 51:5; John 3:6a; Romans 3:10-12; 5:12-14, 20a; 7:14-25

Free grace and works of faith: Ezekiel 18:25-26; John 1:12-13; 3:6b; Acts 5:31; Romans 5:6-8, 18; 6:15-16, 23; 10:6-8; 11:22; 1 Corinthians 2:9-14; 10:1-12; 2 Corinthians 5:18-19; Galatians 5:6; Ephesians 2:8-10; Philippians 2:12-13; Colossians 1:21-23; 2 Timothy 4:10a; Titus 2:11-14; Hebrews 2:1-3; 3:12-15; 6:4-6; 10:26-31; James 2:18-22; 2 Peter 1:10-11; 2:20-22)

VIII. Repentance

8. We believe the Spirit of God gives to all who will repent the gracious help of penitence of heart and hope of mercy, that they may believe unto pardon and spiritual life. Repentance, which is a sincere and thorough change of the mind in regard to sin, involving a sense of personal guilt and a voluntary turning away from sin, is demanded of all who have by act or purpose become sinners against God.

We believe that all persons may fall from grace and apostatize and, unless they repent of their sins, be hopelessly and eternally lost. We believe that regenerate persons need not return to sin but may live in unbroken fellowship with God through the power of the indwelling Holy Spirit who bears witness with our spirits that we are children of God.

(2 Chronicles 7:14; Psalms 32:5-6; 51:1-17; Isaiah 55:6-7; Jeremiah 3:12-14; Ezekiel 18:30-32; 33:14-16; Mark 1:14-15; Luke 3:1-14; 13:1-5; 18:9-14; Acts 2:38; 3:19; 5:31; 17:30-31; 26:16-18; Romans 2:4; 2 Corinthians 7:8-11; 1 Thessalonians 1:9; 2 Peter 3:9)

IX. Justification, Regeneration, and Adoption

9. We believe that justification is the gracious and judicial act of God by which He grants full pardon of all guilt and complete release from the penalty of sins committed, and acceptance as righteous, to all who believe on Jesus Christ and receive Him as Lord and Savior.

9.1 We believe that regeneration, or the new birth, is that gracious work of God whereby the moral nature of the repentant believer is spiritually quickened and given a distinctively spiritual life, capable of faith, love, and obedience.

9.2 We believe that adoption is that gracious act of God by which the justified and regenerated believer is constituted a child of God.

9.3 We believe that justification, regeneration, and adoption are simultaneous in the experience of seekers after God and are received by faith, preceded by repentance; and that to this work and state of grace the Holy Spirit bears witness.

(Luke 18:14; John 1:12-13; 3:3-8; 5:24; Acts 13:39; Romans 1:17; 3:21-26, 28; 4:5-9, 17-25; 5:1, 16-19; 6:4; 7:6; 8:1, 15-17; 1 Corinthians 1:30; 6:11; 2 Corinthians 5:17-21; Galatians 2:16-21; 3:1-14,

26; 4:4-7; Ephesians 1:6-7; 2:1, 4-5; Philippians 3:3-9; Colossians 2:13; Titus 3:4-7; 1 Peter 1:23; 1 John 1:9; 3:1-2, 9; 4:7; 5:1, 9-13, 18)

X. Christian Holiness and Entire Sanctification

10. We believe that sanctification is the work of God which transforms believers into the likeness of Christ. It is wrought by God's grace through the Holy Spirit in initial sanctification, or regeneration (simultaneous with justification), entire sanctification, and the continued perfecting work of the Holy Spirit culminating in glorification. In glorification we are fully conformed to the image of the Son.

We believe that entire sanctification is that act of God, subsequent to regeneration, by which believers are made free from original sin, or depravity, and brought into a state of entire devotement to God, and the holy obedience of love made perfect.

It is wrought by the baptism with or infilling of the Holy Spirit, and comprehends in one experience the cleansing of the heart from sin and the abiding, indwelling presence of the Holy Spirit, empowering the believer for life and service. Entire sanctification is provided by the blood of Jesus, is wrought instantaneously by grace through faith, preceded by entire consecration; and to this work and state of grace the Holy Spirit bears witness.

This experience is also known by various terms representing its different phases, such as "Christian perfection," "perfect love," "heart unity," "the baptism with or infilling of the Holy Spirit," "the fullness of the blessing," and "Christian holiness."

10.1 We believe that there is a marked distinction between a pure heart and a mature character. The former is obtained in an instant, the result of entire sanctification; the latter is the result of growth in grace.

We believe that the grace of entire sanctification includes the divine impulse to grow in grace as a Christlike disciple. However, this impulse must be consciously nurtured, and careful attention given to the requisites and processes of spiritual development and improvement in Christlikeness of character and personality. Without such purposeful endeavor, one's witness may be impaired and the grace itself frustrated and ultimately lost.

Participating in the means of grace, especially the fellowship, disciplines, and sacraments of the Church, believers grow in grace and in wholehearted love to God and neighbor.

(Jeremiah 31:31-34; Ezekiel 36:25-27; Malachi 3:2-3; Matthew 3:11-12; Luke 3:16-17; John 7:37-39; 14:15-23; 17:6-20; Acts 1:5; 2:1-4; 15:8-9; Romans 6:11-13, 19; 8:1-4, 8-14; 12:1-2; 2 Corinthians 6:14–7:1; Galatians 2:20; 5:16-25; Ephesians 3:14-21; 5:17-18, 25-27; Philippians 3:10-15; Colossians 3:1-17; 1 Thessalonians 5:23-24; Hebrews 4:9-11; 10:10-17; 12:1-2; 13:12; 1 John 1:7, 9)

("Christian perfection," "perfect love": Deuteronomy 30:6; Matthew 5:43-48; 22:37-40; Romans 12:9-21; 13:8-10; 1 Corinthians 13; Philippians 3:10-15; Hebrews 6:1; 1 John 4:17-18

"Heart purity": Matthew 5:8; Acts 15:8-9; 1 Peter 1:22; 1 John 3:3

"Baptism with the Holy Spirit": Jeremiah 31:31-34; Ezekiel 36:25-27; Malachi 3:2-3; Matthew 3:11-12; Luke 3:16-17; Acts 1:5; 2:1-4; 15:8-9

"Fullness of the blessing": Romans 15:29

"Christian holiness": Matthew 5:1–7:29; John 15:1-11; Romans 12:1–15:3; 2 Corinthians 7:1; Ephesians 4:17–5:20; Philippians 1:9-11; 3:12-15; Colossians 2:20–3:17; 1 Thessalonians 3:13; 4:7-8; 5:23; 2 Timothy 2:19-22; Hebrews 10:19-25; 12:14; 13:20-21; 1 Peter 1:15-16; 2 Peter 1:1-11; 3:18; Jude 20-21)

XI. The Church

11. We believe in the Church, the community that confesses Jesus Christ as Lord, the covenant people of God made new in Christ, the Body of Christ called together by the Holy Spirit through the Word.

God calls the Church to express its life in the unity and fellowship of the Spirit; in worship through the preaching of the Word, observance of the sacraments, and ministry in His name; by obedience to Christ, holy living, and mutual accountability.

The mission of the Church in the world is to share in the redemptive and reconciling ministry of Christ in the power of the Spirit. The Church fulfills its mission by making disciples through evangelism, education, showing compassion, working for justice, and bearing witness to the kingdom of God.

The Church is a historical reality that organizes itself in culturally conditioned forms, exists both as local congregations and as a universal body, and also sets apart persons called of God for specific ministries. God calls the Church to live under His rule in anticipation of the consummation at the coming of our Lord Jesus Christ.

(Exodus 19:3; Jeremiah 31:33; Matthew 8:11; 10:7; 16:13-19, 24; 18:15-20; 28:19-20; John 17:14-26; 20:21-23; Acts 1:7-8; 2:32-47; 6:1-2; 13:1; 14:23; Romans 2:28-29; 4:16; 10:9-15; 11:13-32; 12:1-8; 15:1-3; 1 Corinthians 3:5-9; 7:17; 11:1, 17-33; 12:3, 12-31; 14:26-40; 2 Corinthians 5:11–6:1; Galatians 5:6, 13-14; 6:1-5, 15; Ephesians 4:1-17; 5:25-27; Philippians 2:1-16; 1 Thessalonians 4:1-12; 1 Timothy 4:13; Hebrews 10:19-25; 1 Peter 1:1-2, 13; 2:4-12, 21; 4:1-2, 10-11; 1 John 4:17; Jude 24; Revelation 5:9-10)

XII. Baptism

12. We believe that Christian baptism, commanded by our Lord, is a sacrament signifying acceptance of the benefits of the atonement and incorporation into the Body of Christ. Baptism is a means of grace proclaiming faith in Jesus Christ as Savior. It is to be administered to believers indicating their full purpose of obedience in holiness and righteousness. As participants in the new covenant, young children and the morally innocent may be baptized upon request of parents or guardians. The church shall give assurance of Christian training. Baptism may be administered by sprinkling, pouring, or immersion.

(Matthew 3:1-7; 28:16-20; Acts 2:37-41; 8:35-39; 10:44-48; 16:29-34; 19:1-6; Romans 6:3-4; Galatians 3:26-28; Colossians 2:12; 1 Peter 3:18-22)

XIII. The Lord's Supper

13. We believe that the Communion Supper instituted by our Lord and Savior Jesus Christ is a sacrament, proclaiming His life, sufferings, sacrificial death, resurrection, and the hope of His coming again. The Lord's Supper is a means of grace in which Christ is present by the Spirit. All are invited to participate by faith in Christ and be renewed in life, salvation, and in unity as the Church. All are to come in reverent appreciation of its significance, and by it show forth the Lord's death until He comes. Those who have faith in Christ and love for the saints are invited by Christ to participate as often as possible.

(Exodus 12:1-14; Matthew 26:26-29; Mark 14:22-25; Luke 22:17-20; John 6:28-58; 1 Corinthians 10:14-21; 11:23-32)

XIV. Divine Healing

14. We believe in the biblical doctrine of divine healing and urge our people to offer the prayer of faith for the healing of the sick. We also believe God heals through the means of medical science.

(2 Kings 5:1-19; Psalm 103:1-5; Matthew 4:23-24; 9:18-35; John 4:46-54; Acts 5:12-16; 9:32-42; 14:8-15; 1 Corinthians 12:4-11; 2 Corinthians 12:7-10; James 5:13-16)

XV. Second Coming of Christ

15. We believe that the Lord Jesus Christ will come again; that we who are alive at His coming shall not precede them that are asleep in Christ Jesus; but that, if we are abiding in Him, we shall be caught up with the risen saints to meet the Lord in the air, so that we shall ever be with the Lord.

(Matthew 25:31-46; John 14:1-3; Acts 1:9-11; Philippians 3:20-21; 1 Thessalonians 4:13-18; Titus 2:11-14; Hebrews 9:26-28; 2 Peter 3:3-15; Revelation 1:7-8; 22:7-20)

XVI. Resurrection, Judgment, and Destiny

16. We believe in the resurrection of the dead, that the bodies both of the just and of the unjust shall be raised to life and united with their spirits—"they that have done good, unto the resurrection of life; and they that have done evil, unto the resurrection of damnation."

16.1. We believe in future judgment in which every person shall appear before God to be judged according to his or her deeds in this life.

16.2. We believe that glorious and everlasting life is assured to all who savingly believe in, and obediently follow, Jesus Christ our Lord; and that the finally impenitent shall suffer eternally in hell.

(Genesis 18:25; 1 Samuel 2:10; Psalm 50:6; Isaiah 26:19; Daniel 12:2-3; Matthew 25:31-46; Mark 9:43-48; Luke 16:19-31; 20:27-38; John 3:16-18; 5:25-29; 11:21-27; Acts 17:30-31; Romans 2:1-16; 14:7-12; 1 Corinthians 15:12-58; 2 Corinthians 5:10; 2 Thessalonians 1:5-10; Revelation 20:11-15; 22:1-15)

4. ORGANIZATION
LOCAL
AND
GLOBAL

The Church of the Nazarene has a distinctive organization. It combines the benefits of local authority with the blessings of a larger affiliation. Individual churches have considerable freedom without being independent of one another or of the whole.

Each local Nazarene church is part of the global family of Nazarene congregations. Each church is expected to follow the same rules, regulations, and procedures that are followed by every other Nazarene congregation in the world. The ethical and moral standards of each Nazarene church are the same as those in other Nazarene churches. All Nazarene churches are united by a core set of beliefs and also by a system of governance that has proved to be durable across many cultures and for more than a century.

At the same time, there is significant and real freedom in each congregation. Churches choose their own pastors, elect their own leaders, and make their own decisions about worship styles, decor, and much more. You can find many types of worship at Nazarene churches, ranging from contemporary to more traditional. Worship styles are one obvious example of the various ways that individual Nazarene churches can express themselves.

Although this little book cannot examine every single detail of how Nazarene churches are organized, we'll do our best to sketch out the overall picture in this chapter. In the next few pages we will look at how the global Church of the Nazarene is organized and how each individual church fits into the larger picture as God's kingdom advances around the world.

The Local Church

The local church is at the heart of the Church of the Nazarene. It is here, within each congregation, that people grow up in Christ and become mature. It is here, within each community of faith, that men and women discover their spiritual gifts and begin serving others with gladness. It is here that each person lives out his or her purpose, fulfilling God's plan.

Each local church is led by a senior (or lead) pastor. A pastor is elected by church members after having been nominated by the church board with the approval of the district superintendent (see next section). The lead pastor serves the primary role as the spiritual leader of the congregation. Additionally, since congregations raise money and make financial choices, the lead pastor also has administrative and legal roles in the congregation. One of the passages from the Bible that describes the ministry and the role of the local church pastor is 1 Peter 5:1-4:

To the elders among you, I appeal as a fellow elder and a witness of Christ's sufferings who also will share in the glory to be revealed: Be shepherds of God's flock that is under your care, watching over them—not because you must, but because you are willing, as God wants you to be; not pursuing dishonest gain, but eager to serve; not lording it over those entrusted to you, but being examples to the flock. And when the Chief Shepherd appears, you will receive the crown of glory that will never fade away.

The lead pastor's duties of ministry include preaching and teaching God's Word, administering the sacraments, training people in Christian discipleship and service, and the shepherding work of watching over God's flock. The duties of administration include being the chair of the church board. These duties are more fully explained in the most recent edition of the *Manual* of the Church of the Nazarene.

Periodically a pastor's ministry is evaluated and reviewed. The presiding district superintendent leads the church board in consideration of the ministry effectiveness and leadership qualities of the pastor, as well as the overall health and perceived progress of the church. Pastoral reviews are prescribed in the *Manual* and occur every few years on a schedule coordinated by the district superintendent.

Larger churches may have multiple pastors, or associate ministers, for purposes such as music ministry, children's ministry, youth ministry, ministry to senior adults, and family ministry. The lead pastor requests permission from the district superintendent to hire additional staff. With permission granted, the pastor then screens and nominates the associate pastor(s). The nominee(s) must be approved by the district superintendent and then elected by the local church board.

When a pastor leaves or resigns, or whenever there is a vacancy in the lead pastoral role, the district superintendent guides the church board in the process of searching for their next pastor. The district superintendent may bring the names of appropriate candidates to the board for consideration; the local church may also have names it wishes to consider. After a careful and prayerful process involving the district superintendent and the church board, eventually a pastoral candidate is officially presented to the congregation for their consideration. The congregation together then votes on the potential candidate.

In very small churches, the presiding district superintendent may appoint the next pastor when there is a vacancy. Procedural guidance for such cases is described in detail in the *Manual*. In general, the district superintendent will attempt to gain feedback and evaluation from the church board prior to the appointment of a new pastor. Every effort is made to locate a pastor with the appropriate capacity for ministry and evident gifts for leadership and service to the local church.

Together with the pastor, the local church board makes decisions about the direction and future of its congregation. Each church elects members of the church board on a regular basis, a process that is described in the *Manual*. The general and required qualifications for a church board member include clear evidence of salvation and growth in Christ, the profession of entire sanctification, demonstrated personal maturity and self-control, appropriate humility and wisdom in leadership, and active encouragement of the church and its ministries as displayed by consistent attendance and faithful financial support. Clearly the candidates for potential inclusion on the church board are held to a higher standard in their Christian walk, with the hope that those who end up in leadership in a local church are godly, mature, humble, and wise.

In healthy churches, the spiritual leadership of the pastor is supported and acknowledged by all. The church board, acting as mature Christian leaders, supports the ministry of the church and the ministers who serve it. Healthy churches are a wonderful example to all—both Christians and nonbelievers—because they operate in a spirit of unity, recognizing the spiritual leadership of the pastor.

The District Church

In the Church of the Nazarene, individual congregations come together as districts for purposes that include advancing the gospel, conducting effective ministry to parents and families, and providing opportunities for Christian service.

District boundaries generally reflect geographical closeness and proximity, but the boundaries are also determined by the number of churches found within a local area. Areas with a heavier concentration of Nazarene churches will be broken up into a higher number of geographical districts, while areas with fewer Nazarene churches will spread out their district boundaries to encompass more land. For example, within the United States, the state of Texas is broken up into three districts because of the size of the state relative to the number of Nazarene churches found within it. By contrast, the three states of North Dakota, South Dakota, and Minnesota come together to compose one district that covers all three states. In some parts of the world, an entire nation may be one district.

Each district is led by an elected district superintendent who functions much like a local pastor. The district superintendent has both ministerial and administrative duties. On the ministry side, the district superintendent cares for the spiritual health and well-being of the pastors and ministers (and their families) within the district, functioning in this way as somewhat of a pastor to pastors. The district superintendent also oversees active and robust ministerial training, both for those aspiring to ministry as a calling and to those already serving. On the administrative side, the district superintendent has specific duties that include helping congregations find a new pastor during a vacancy, helping congregations make decisions about major purchases such as buildings and land, and bringing the churches on the district together for common purposes such as ministry to families, youth, and children, or support for missions and expanding evangelism. The specific roles and duties of the district superintendent are defined more fully in the *Manual*.

Just as a local church has both a pastor and a church board, each district has both a district superintendent and a district advisory board. The advisory board consists of an equal number of ordained ministers (clergy) and non-ordained church members (laity) so that the district receives a balanced perspective on church and congregational life in the district. Each district elects persons to the advisory board during annual meetings known as district assemblies.

When churches come together as a district, more can be accomplished. Smaller churches may be unable to create or operate effective youth ministries. Districts typically conduct a youth camp each summer, which is a weeklong program of special events, worship services, and fun designed specifically for adolescents and teens. Districts may also conduct annual children's camps. Additionally, many districts host an annual family camp that features solid Bible teaching, energetic worship services, and plenty of enjoyable activities for the whole family.

Churches on a district may come together in ministry teams, traveling to support local churches on the district or traveling farther away to conduct short-term mission trips. Often when churches are smaller, groups of churches (or the whole district) will join forces to form what the Church of the Nazarene calls Work and Witness teams. These teams work on specific projects such as building a school or repairing a church, or they may bring a ministry team to lead sports camps for youth, Bible schools for children, or discipleship classes for adults. Serving for only a week or two at a time, Work and Witness teams may travel to far countries or minister and serve closer to home.

While these examples are by no means exhaustive, they serve to show the power of joining together as districts in order to minister in ways that perhaps a local congregation, especially a smaller one, might not be able to fund, staff, coordinate, or accomplish on its own. Districts are a useful way to accomplish more ministry while training more ministers.

The Regional Church

As the Church of the Nazarene has grown, an additional level of coordination has been established. At one time, there were simply three levels: local, district, and global. A fourth level, situated in hierarchy between district and global and called regional, was added to accommodate the increasing demands of a growing denomination. Regions are not as fully orbed or completely staffed as the other levels of church operation. In general, regional administration primarily involves coordinating mission work and church planting.

As of 2019, there are six world regions in the Church of the Nazarene. These are as follows:

1. USA/Canada, with offices in Lenexa, Kansas

2. Mesoamerica (Central America plus the Caribbean islands), with offices in Panama City, Panama

3. South America (all of the South American continent except for Guyana, Suriname, and French Guiana), with offices in Buenos Aires, Argentina

4. Eurasia (all of Europe, much of Asia, portions of northern Africa, Iceland, and more), with offices in Schaffhausen, Switzerland

5. Asia-Pacific (Southeast Asia, including the island nations plus Australia and New Zealand), with offices in Singapore

6. Africa Region (almost all of the African continent except northern Africa), with offices in Johannesburg, Republic of South Africa

Each of the six regional offices is led by a regional director, elected by the Board of General Superintendents and ratified by the General Board for the church. Regional directors coordinate missional strategies for the territories in their regions. They thus work closely with whichever of the six general superintendents (see next section) currently presides over their regional districts.

The Global Church

The topmost organizational level in the Church of the Nazarene is the global, or general, church. The work of the global church has its base of operations at the Global Ministry Center (GMC), located just outside Kansas City, Missouri, in the suburban community of Lenexa, Kansas. From the GMC, the organizational, financial, and missional life of the worldwide church is coordinated.

The general church gathers once every four years at what is called General Assembly, for the purpose of conducting church business, electing new general superintendents, and amending the *Manual*. Delegates to General Assembly come from the many and diverse places where the Church of the Nazarene has a presence. When attending General Assembly, one will hear many world languages and meet godly, Christlike people from every corner of the globe. Although the primary purpose of General Assembly is to conduct church business, there are also high-energy worship services that feature outstanding preaching and uplifting music and praise. Typically there are also a few events for children and teens, along with several affinity-based gatherings organized by various ministry groups. Attending General Assembly should be on the bucket list for every active member of the Church of the Nazarene!

Currently, each General Assembly is tasked with electing six leaders to serve as general superintendents. Some denominations are led by a single general superintendent; others have several. The Church of the Nazarene, responding to its rapid and consistent growth in so many parts of the world, has gradually expanded to six. Recent studies and commissions have affirmed that at least six general superintendents are still needed and useful.

General superintendents, elected by the General Assembly, function as pastors to the global church. They travel constantly, attending district assemblies and presiding over church business meetings as well as approving and ordaining new pastors and ministers. The role is intended to be one primarily of spiritual leadership, yet with a rapidly expanding denomination that faces multiple challenges, there are inevitable administrative duties that also must be served.

Together and collectively, the six elected general superintendents are known as the Board of General Superintendents (BGS). Although each one of the six has separate areas of responsibility, at times the BGS may issue statements on key issues of doctrine or practice, articulating the Nazarene response. One of the requirements for being elected as a general superintendent is being an ordained minister in good standing in the Church of the Nazarene.

Just as a local church has both a pastor and a church board, and a district has a district superintendent and a district advisory board, the global church is served by its six general superintendents and also by the members of a group known as the

General Board. The members of the General Board are elected at the General Assembly. The size of the board has expanded due to church growth; as of 2019, there are fifty-three members of the General Board. Between General Assemblies, this board carries out the corporate business of the global church. Always changing, roughly half of the current composition of the General Board consists of members from outside North America. The General Board is made up of district superintendents, pastors, and laypeople, as well representatives from Global Missions, Nazarene higher education, and Nazarene youth ministry.

Some Important Church Ministries

The general church encompasses several distinct ministries. Each is tasked with coordinating and resourcing its specific area of responsibility. There are three primary general ministries:

Nazarene Missions International (NMI)

This ministry raises support and awareness for Nazarene missions and missionaries. Each local church elects an NMI leader and an NMI council or board, which function to raise awareness and support within the local church. From the local church, the next step is the district. Each district elects an NMI leader and an NMI council or board, which raise awareness and support for missions at the district level. Finally, at the global level, the General Assembly elects an NMI leader and an NMI council or board, which coordinate missions work at the worldwide level. Typically the globally elected NMI leader maintains an office at the Global Ministry Center of the Church of the Nazarene in Lenexa, Kansas.

Nazarene Youth International (NYI)

This ministry focuses on the youth—primarily middle school and high school students, with some additional support for college students and young adults. Much like NMI, NYI exists at local, district, and global levels of the church. Local churches elect their own NYI president, who coordinates ministry to youth. Districts elect a district NYI president, often a youth pastor from a church on the district, who coordinates district-wide ministry to students and youth. Finally, the General Assembly elects a global NYI president. In recent years there has been a de-emphasis on NYI boards or councils. Typically, a local Nazarene church will have an NYI president but no corresponding NYI board or council. At the district and global levels, there are still functioning boards or councils, although the roles are advisory in nature rather than legal or administrative.

Sunday School and Discipleship Ministries International (SDMI)

This ministry facilitates disciple making and equips families for growing in their faith. Like NMI and NYI, SDMI is replicated at the local, district, and global levels with elected leaders of each. Like NMI, SDMI typically has a board or council at each level as well. SDMI is tasked with diverse responsibilities such as curriculum development, Bible study, ministry to families, and ministry to single adults. SDMI is the broadest of the general ministries and perhaps also the most difficult to succinctly define. It emerged originally as the Sunday school arm of the church, which is still reflected in the name. Across the years, the mission and mandate have expanded broadly, well beyond the hour of educational time that typically occurs on a Sunday morning. Today's SDMI features webcasts, podcasts, and conferences at the global level and often conferences and seminars at the district level. Like NMI, the global director of SDMI has typically maintained an office at the church's Global Ministry Center in Lenexa, Kansas.

This, then, is a bird's-eye view of the Church of the Nazarene as it operates throughout the world. It is first of all a network of local congregations, grouped into districts to work collectively and gathered into a global church united by common beliefs, practices, and organizational structure.

As a new member of the Church of the Nazarene, you'll want to attend your own congregation's annual meeting, watching and learning as business is conducted and decisions are made. You might also enjoy attending your district's assembly, which always includes high-quality worship and preaching. Even if you are not elected to be an official delegate to your district's assembly, you might enjoy attending as a learning experience, or simply to experience the worship, the praise, and the celebration of what God has done on the district.

5. MEMBERSHIP

BEING A CHURCH MEMBER

Remember John Wesley, whom we mentioned in chapter 2? Wesley's primary focus was this: How can we help people grow and mature spiritually? What approach should we use? What methods actually work? As we noted already, John Wesley's methods for helping people grow in Christ started the movement that is still known today as Methodism. And, as you have already learned, the Church of the Nazarene is part of the Methodist-Wesleyan tradition, or what is often referred to as the Wesleyan-holiness tradition. Our goal is to help Christians grow spiritually so that they live radically transformed lives.

Church membership greatly encourages this growth and radical transformation. Becoming a church member places you in a close-knit fellowship of love and accountability where opportunities to grow spiritually and live a radically transformed life are multiplied. Committing to a church through membership opens the way to increased expressions of love to God and neighbor as you serve and are nurtured in the company of other Christ followers.

In the next few pages, we will talk about what membership in your local Nazarene church means. Since this chapter is mostly a brief overview, we encourage you to meet with your local Nazarene pastor and join the next membership class, which is simply an informational session (or series of sessions) to help you make an informed choice.

For the purposes of this chapter, let's start with the Bible. This passage from Ephesians 3:14-19 talks about growing in Christ, which is one of the primary purposes for joining and becoming a member of a church:

> For this reason I kneel before the Father, from whom every family in heaven and on earth derives its name. I pray that out of his glorious riches he may strengthen you with power through his Spirit in your inner being, so that Christ may dwell in your hearts through faith. And I pray that you, being rooted and established in love, may have power, together with all the Lord's holy people, to grasp how wide and long and high and deep is the love of Christ, and to know this love that surpasses knowledge—that you may be filled to the measure of all the fullness of God.

This is what it's all about. As Paul writes to the believers at Ephesus, the key principle is "being rooted and established in love" and learning "how wide and long and high and deep" Christ's love for us really is. This is the process of growing in our spiritual lives and in our understanding of God's will for us. This is the pathway we begin to walk when we decide to become a member of a Nazarene church.

This is good news! And the good news continues when we realize that we will not be walking this pathway alone. God will help us, and we will also have the help of a whole new group of family and friends—the other members of our local Church of the Nazarene. No one has to grow alone or figure things out alone. Each one of us can become part of a growing, healthy, accountable fellowship in which no one judges the others but each one encourages and supports the others. Wouldn't you love to be part of a group like that? You can be, if you decide to pursue church membership.

Now, with that overall understanding in mind, let's look at becoming a church member through the lenses of these four broad categories of what church members do and how church members choose to live. Remember, these are broad *descriptions* of church membership rather than *prescriptions* about church membership.

Gathering

Church members get together on a regular basis. As the old Thanksgiving hymn says, "We gather together to ask the Lord's blessing."[2] This is not just a great image but also an accurate description of what church members do. Church members meet together regularly for worship and learning, for wise Bible teaching and prayer, and for ministry to children or teens or families or individuals.

Your local Nazarene church probably gathers on Sundays. Like many other churches, the common gathering times are on Sunday mornings between nine and eleven. Yet you can find Nazarene churches that intentionally avoid Sunday mornings, timing their weekly gatherings so that busy parents and families can have a day of rest even on Sundays. These churches may have a weekly worship service that begins at four or six on a Sunday afternoon or evening. Other Nazarene churches may offer a Saturday night service, either as their regular weekly gathering time or as one of several regular options. There are some Nazarene churches, typically among the larger congregations, that choose to offer the same sermon and worship experience three or four different times during the weekend, giving busy churchgoers a wide range of choices. Even smaller churches may offer two separate services on Sunday

---

2. "We Gather Together," in *Sing to the Lord* (Kansas City: Lillenas, 1993), no. 767.

so that early risers and those who start the day a bit later can attend at a time that fits their schedule.

Church members gather. They make church attendance a priority, not because it is required, but because it reveals where their hearts are. Church members really do want to grow spiritually. They really do want to become more Christlike and godly. They really do want to learn how to serve. Here is wise advice from the New Testament: "And let us consider how we may spur one another on toward love and good deeds, not giving up meeting together, as some are in the habit of doing, but encouraging one another" (Hebrews 10:24-25a).

Church members get together to support each other, to encourage each other, to learn about God, and to draw closer to God. As the saying goes, "There are no Lone Rangers in Christianity." What that means is that Christians have gathered together since the very beginning. The disciples gathered after Christ's death. The early Christians gathered in an upper room to pray, waiting for God's Holy Spirit. From the first days of Christianity to these current days, believers in Jesus Christ make gathering together a priority in their lives.

Giving

Giving is a way of acknowledging that God owns everything. For Christians, this idea is especially meaningful. New Testament writers declare that we belong to Christ, having been purchased by his sacrifice (e.g., Matthew 20:28; Romans 14:8; 1 Corinthians 6:20; 7:22-23; Titus 2:13-14). So all we have and all we are belong to God, and we are to give freely, cheerfully, and lovingly as an act of worship and thanksgiving to God (see 2 Corinthians 8:1-15; 9:6-11). We are to give to help the needy and to support the work of the church. We are to give of ourselves and our resources. It is not just what we give but that we give from a heart of love for God and neighbor.

Because we will discuss serving, or the giving of our time, later in this chapter, we will concentrate on financial giving here. Members of the Church of the Nazarene give tithes and offerings regularly to support the church's ministry. A tithe is a tenth of one's increase—income or gifts received—and is mentioned in Scripture in a number of places. Here are several examples from the Old Testament: Abraham gave God's priest a tenth of his gain from a victorious battle as a thank-you to God (Genesis 14). Jacob promised to give a tenth of his increase to God following a pivotal experience with God (28:10-22).

Malachi stressed that Israel's failure to give tithes and offerings demonstrated a lack of faithfulness to God (Malachi 3:8-12). But the prophet Amos asserted that without care for the poor and needy, giving tithes and offerings becomes a hollow practice (Amos 4). The New Testament has fewer references to tithing, but the words of Jesus, like those of Amos, unite the practice of tithing—or expressing love and faithfulness to God—with showing love and care for others: "Woe to you, teachers of the law and Pharisees, you hypocrites! You give a tenth of your spices—mint, dill and cumin. But you have neglected the more important matters of the law— justice, mercy and faithfulness. You should have practiced the latter, without neglecting the former" (Matthew 23:23).

The *Manual* has these words to say about tithing: Storehouse tithing is a scriptural and practical performance of faithfully and regularly placing the tithe into that church to which the member belongs. Therefore, the financing of the church shall be based on the plan of storehouse tithing, and the local Church of the Nazarene shall be regarded by all of its people as the storehouse. All who are a part of the Church of the Nazarene are urged to contribute faithfully one-tenth of all their increase as a minimum financial obligation to the Lord and freewill offerings in addition as God has prospered them for the support of the whole church, local, district, educational, and general. The tithe, provided to the local Church of the Nazarene, shall be considered a priority over all other giving opportunities which God may lay upon the hearts of His faithful stewards, in support of the whole church. (Para. 32.1)

Comparing Old Testament and New Testament practices, author and educator Wes Tracy observes, "The Old Testament minimum was a tenth. But the New Testament says 'See that you also excel in this grace of giving' (2 Corinthians 8:7, NIV). Surely excelling means something different from the minimum requirement of Old Testament law. . . . Perhaps we should think of *how much* we can give and not *how little*."[3]

Giving to the church is one expression of our faithfulness and commitment to God and the gospel of Christ. We give to the church to pay the bills, to support the pastors and staff who serve in ministry, and to help advance the kingdom. Giving to the

---

3. Tracy, Wesley D., "The Tithing Tradition," in *The Christian's Guide to Financial Freedom* (Kansas City: Beacon Hill Press of Kansas City, 2000), https://s3.amazonaws.com /media.cloversites.com/f3/f3f6996c-a3de-41ee-936e-2af82 59792c0/documents/The_Tithing_Tradition.pdf.

needy is also an essential part of Christlike living. As we give cheerfully, worshipfully, and generously, we open up ourselves to God's transforming presence. By giving, we affirm God's ownership of all creation and our dependence on God and we allow God to work through us to bestow blessings on the disadvantaged. By being an avenue of God's blessings to others, we ourselves are blessed with the joy and fullness of a deeper relationship with God.

Learning

When church members gather, learning is one of their top priorities. Most of us know only so much of the Bible. Most of us don't have it memorized. In fact, many of us, especially those of us who are new to church, can't even find a book of the Bible without using the table of contents! But that's okay. After all, a table of contents was printed in the Bible to help us.

You don't need to be embarrassed about how little Scripture you know or how few Bible verses you can recite from memory. It's not a contest. Yet when church members gather together, one of the highest priorities is learning God's Word.

This learning can happen in several settings. It can happen in small groups or Sunday school classes. Group leaders or Sunday school teachers guide participants through scriptural-based studies and discussions. In these group gatherings, a wide range of topics can be covered in detail. Moreover, these gatherings provide excellent opportunities for fellowship and friendship as participants grow and learn together.

Learning also happens during worship through preaching and teaching. Pastors are trained in interpreting, preaching, and teaching the Bible. Listening carefully to a sermon, and following along in a Bible as the pastor preaches, is an effective way to gain greater understanding. Life-changing insights from the Word of God often come while attending to a sermon.

As a practical tip, you may want to consider getting a study Bible to facilitate your own learning. Study Bibles typically include more notes of explanation than bare-bones Bibles. These notes reference other Scriptures or explain key ideas that may be unfamiliar. There are dozens of study Bibles to choose from; ask your pastor for a recommendation.

While you are talking to your pastor, ask about the different translations of the Bible. Many Nazarenes tend to favor the *New International Version* (NIV), although you can find many different translations being used in Nazarene services.

Apps, available for your smartphone, can help you explore Bible translations and get to know the Bible. If you attend a Nazarene church service almost anywhere in the world today, you will find believers who are reading God's Word on their phones while the pastor reads and teaches from the pulpit.

Serving

The fourth and final category we will consider in this chapter is serving. Church members are not spectators who sit back and watch as a church service or event happens. Church members understand that part of what it means to join a church community is to find a way to serve and help.

Serving and helping is a deeply ingrained Nazarene tradition. Whether it is feeding the hungry, raising money for missions, or supporting a rescue effort to free victims of human trafficking, Nazarenes find ways to serve and help. In many churches there is a constant need for someone to work in the nursery, caring for babies while mothers and fathers attend worship or Sunday school. Although changing diapers is not exactly glamorous work, it is necessary, even in the church! It is also a huge help for busy parents who do plenty of diaper changing all week. The chance to come to church—to praise, worship, study, learn, and fellowship while someone else cares for the crying baby or changes a diaper—is priceless.

You can serve and help by parking cars, painting classrooms, cooking food, visiting the sick in the hospital, and in many other ways. There is no one way that is the best way to serve. How you serve will be as individual and unique as you are! Just remember that you can always find places where more help is needed and where a little extra effort at just the right time can make a meaningful difference in someone's life.

Since we've been looking at verses from the book of Hebrews already in this chapter, here's a relevant passage about serving and helping: "Through Jesus, therefore, let us continually offer to God a sacrifice of praise—the fruit of lips that openly profess his name. And do not forget to do good and to share with others, for with such sacrifices God is pleased" (13:15-16). These are two of many Bible verses that remind us to serve and help. Whether we are serving food at a homeless shelter, volunteering for a mission trip, or helping to plan a youth night or special activity, there are many ways to serve.

As church members we are part of a family; we are members of the same team. We understand that each person shares as he or she is able and that each person plays a unique role in the overall success of the mission. Maybe you're a cook and not a Bible teacher. Maybe you are a bus driver and not a guitar player. Just because your specific way of helping may be less dramatic or less visible than that of others doesn't mean it isn't valuable. Every person has a way to serve and help.

One elderly widow was sorrowful to be physically frail and nearly blind. She told her pastor, "All I can do now is pray for people."

The pastor thanked her from a sincere heart. After all, what a gift! How wonderful to have a mature saint praying for people in the church. If all you can do is pray, thank you for praying!

In these four ways—gathering, giving, learning, and serving—church members express their support for God's ongoing mission and God's purposes. Through these ways and others, church members demonstrate their commitment and their faithfulness.

Becoming a church member is a way to become more responsible and mature. It is an opportunity to place greater attention on serving others. Learning to serve others in humility is perhaps the best way to follow the clear and consistent example of Jesus Christ.

Here is how Paul described Christ's example to the church gathered at Philippi. Paul was clear about Christ's behavior and why we should follow it:

Therefore if you have any encouragement from being united with Christ, if any comfort from his love, if any common sharing in the Spirit, if any tenderness and compassion, then make my joy complete by being like-minded, having the same love, being one in spirit and of one mind. Do nothing out of selfish ambition or vain conceit. Rather, in humility value others above yourselves, not looking to your own interests but each of you to the interests of the others. (Philippians 2:1-4)

What a great description of serving and helping! We see it in the life of Jesus Christ; we also see it in the lives of those who follow him still today.

6. CHRISTIAN LIFE
LIVING A
GODLY LIFE

In this short chapter we will take a look at some primary ingredients of the godly life. We've seen a few of these already when we talked about how church members gather, give, learn, and serve. Those were mostly concerned with what the godly life looks like in public. But what about how it looks in private?

Prayer

A godly life includes a lot of prayer. If you're not a morning person, please relax. Becoming a Christian doesn't mean you have to start setting your alarm for four o'clock every day to have a two-hour prayer session. The point is to pray; it's not about the time of day. You can pray in the evening or the middle of the night! The idea of prayer is not only to talk to God but also to wait and linger in God's presence, gaining a deeper appreciation of who God is. Some people do this while listening to music. Others spend time in prayer while walking or hiking outdoors. And others prefer to pray in the quiet of their bedroom or office. Methods, places, and times for prayer vary a lot from person to person. What works for you?

We know a busy pastor who conducts his prayer life on his computer. He types out his prayers for people daily, at a time that works for him. Those people never see the typed prayer lists; they never even know he has prayed. When he is done praying for the day, he just deletes the file. He argues that, as a visual person, it helps him to see his prayers right there on the screen in front of him. He also says the typing process helps him focus and pray more effectively.

A busy mom we know prays as part of her daily commute. She spends a lot of time in the family SUV taking kids to school and to soccer practice, traveling to and from work, and driving many other places. "I live in my car," she told us with a bright smile. "So why shouldn't I pray in my car? For me, that's about the only place I have some real privacy—*after* dropping the kids off, of course." For some people, time alone in a vehicle is about the only quiet or private time they get all day. For these people, praying in the car makes a lot of sense.

As we learn to love and appreciate God, we will definitely want to spend time in the presence of God. Prayer is a natural outgrowth of our love for God. We just need to find the timing, the rhythm, and, to some extent, the location that work for us so that we can pray effectively and sincerely.

Studying God's Word

Living a godly life includes learning everything you can about God, and that means studying God's

Word. Moreover, studying the Bible is another way to deepen your relationship with God. As with prayer, Bible study is a means of grace—that is, it is a practice through which God works to nurture us and conform us to the likeness of Christ; we make ourselves available to God's gracious and transforming presence as we prayerfully study the Bible.

As you begin to explore the Bible, you may want to consult your pastor about the different approaches you can take. For example, you could study the Bible in order, from beginning to end, or focus on the daily Scripture readings assigned on a church calendar. You could study different types of biblical literature, such as prophecy, gospels, or letters, or devote time to an in-depth look at one book of the Bible. There are benefits of each approach, and your pastor can help you begin.

As we mentioned in the previous chapter, conferring with your pastor is also an excellent way to learn about the different Bible versions and study Bibles. There are several versions that scholars and students rely on. Along with the *New International Version* (NIV), which we've already identified, there are the *New American Standard Bible* (NASB) and the *New Revised Standard Version* (NRSV). These translations are commonly held to be faithfully and carefully translated editions of the Bible. Your pastor can tell you more about these versions and others; he or she can also introduce you to resources such as commentaries, Bible dictionaries, and Bible atlases.

There are many more methods and tools available for Bible study than can be covered in this book. What is important is that you make Bible study a regular part of your life. Setting aside time to dig deeply into the Scriptures will not only increase your understanding but also strengthen your fellowship with God. Remember, like prayer, serious and prayerful Bible study is an avenue through which God blesses us and remakes us into godly people who live and love as Christ does.

Compassionate Ministry

A godly life includes practicing compassion. The word "compassion" literally means "to suffer with." When you love others, you soon discover that love compels you to get involved. As you become more like Christ, you find yourself responding to the plight of the poor and the homeless, those who experience disasters, and those who are victims of social and moral evils. You find yourself suffering with those who suffer.

The basic idea of compassionate ministry is thus caring about your neighbor in need and then doing something about it. Following Jesus means you tend to notice people, as Jesus did, who are otherwise neglected or overlooked. As you learn about the miracles of Jesus, you'll discover that he spent a lot of time feeding the hungry, healing the sick, and encouraging his followers to care for the poor. Over and over in both the Old Testament and the New Testament, God reveals that he cares about people who are poor, alone, or suffering and that anyone who follows him should do the same.

We find just one of many examples from Scripture in Jeremiah 22:3: "This is what the LORD says: Do what is just and right. Rescue from the hand of the oppressor the one who has been robbed. Do no wrong or violence to the foreigner, the fatherless or the widow, and do not shed innocent blood in this place." This is exactly what "compassionate ministry" means—rescuing those who are suffering from violence, doing no harm to foreigners in the land, and taking good care of orphans and widows. In other words, we are to care for anyone who may not have anyone to rely on. As followers of Jesus Christ, we are to notice where the needs are and then do something to meet them.

Much of the New Testament was written by the apostle Paul, who went from persecuting Christians and opposing Christianity to becoming a true believer and preaching the good news about Jesus all over the known world. The life of Paul is a dramatic testimony to what God's love can do in a human heart. Here is what Paul wrote on the subject of compassionate ministry to the group of Christians who gathered together in Rome: "Rejoice with those who rejoice; mourn with those who mourn. Live in harmony with one another. Do not be proud, but be willing to associate with people of low position. Do not be conceited. Do not repay anyone evil for evil. Be careful to do what is right in the eyes of everyone. If it is possible, as far as it depends on you, live at peace with everyone" (Romans 12:15–18).

Nazarene churches are engaged in compassionate ministries in almost every area of the world. A Nazarene church in Minneapolis stocks and fills a large food pantry and opens it up to the poor and hungry at no charge. A Nazarene church in Banning, California, stocks a full-time clothes closet and opens it up once a week for the neighbors and local community. Caring Nazarenes have helped build a rescue center for the victims of human trafficking near Bucharest, Romania. Others are rescuing trafficking victims in Southern California and urban Oklahoma City. Around the globe, if you locate a Nazarene congregation, you'll find a group of people doing their best to be like Jesus—caring about and helping the poor or the oppressed.

Christian Life and Social Issues

Every four years, the delegates at the General Assembly of the Church of the Nazarene wrestle with tough issues and then prayerfully shape the church's answer to current social questions or problems. For questions about specific issues, you will want to consult your pastor and read the church's official statements in the *Manual,* especially the "Covenant of Christian Conduct," which we have included in the appendix.

Living a godly life means following in the footsteps of Jesus. As we pray, study God's Word, and practice compassion, we make ourselves available to God's transforming presence. The call to godly living is the call to Christlikeness, which is a life of love. Loving God and neighbor as Christ does is our goal, and we move toward this goal as we rehearse this love daily. The words of 2 Peter 1:3-8 express this concept well:

His divine power has given us everything we need for a godly life through our knowledge of him who called us by his own glory and goodness. Through these he has given us his very great and precious promises, so that through them you may participate in the divine nature, having escaped the corruption in the world caused by evil desires.

For this very reason, make every effort to add to your faith goodness; and to goodness, knowledge; and to knowledge, self-control; and to self-control, perseverance; and to perseverance, godliness; and to godliness, mutual affection; and to mutual affection, love. For if you possess these qualities in increasing measure, they will keep you from being ineffective and unproductive in your knowledge of our Lord Jesus Christ. God empowers us to live a godly life, and we are to pursue it by encouraging the qualities of that life, beginning with faith and culminating with Christ-like love. May God's love richly surround and transform each one of us as we walk in the steps of Jesus.

7. IDENTITY
FROM
GOOD
TO
GREAT

Welcome to the Church of the Nazarene. For more than a century of church life, we've been doing our best to be a beacon of God's light and love in a hurting world. There's never been a better time for God's people to get involved in serving and helping than right now. One of our founders, Dr. Phineas Bresee, pointed the way for the church to be directly involved in solving or at least alleviating the biggest social problems of its day. Bresee invested his own life significantly in Los Angeles, daily ministering to and serving the poor and needy. Today you can find Nazarene volunteers and Nazarene pastors reaching out to the hurting and the hopeless in some of the world's largest cities.

Nazarenes are making a difference in many world areas and in diverse categories of missions and relief work. You can find Nazarenes on the front lines rescuing the victims of human trafficking in Southern California, Eastern Europe, and many other places where God's light is so desperately needed. You can find Nazarenes building schools and hospitals and churches, literally all over the world. The continent of Africa will never be the same because of the committed and caring Nazarenes who have served and helped there. Across the decades, these dedicated workers have built medical centers that continue to demonstrate state-of-the-art health care in some of the most impoverished places on the planet. From the very beginning, the Nazarene ethos has been to go out into the world to help and serve.

Nazarenes have built campus locations worldwide for colleges, universities, Bible schools, and seminaries. The USA/Canada Region has eleven Nazarene institutions, college level and higher, with a total collective enrollment of more than eighteen thousand students. Each year, graduates depart from these Nazarene schools, taking on the mission of making the world a better place through Christian preaching, teaching, and living. You can find similar Nazarene schools in Africa and Asia, in Central and South America, and in Europe. One such school, European Nazarene College, has built numerous local learning centers in many of the nations of Western and Eastern Europe, uniting students toward a common purpose while allowing those students to remain in the countries where they already reside and work. This model of diversified education is working very well across Europe and beyond.

Nazarenes who may never become pastors or missionaries are discovering that they, too, can help. Many Nazarenes—from Korea to Kenya, from Alabama to Alaska—are taking their annual vacation time to go and work elsewhere. They come together to form Work and Witness teams that may serve and help near home or in distant world areas. For a week or two each year, these caring volunteers come alongside missionaries and local pastors to add their energy, vibrancy, spiritual gifts, and prayers to a variety of ministry settings. Whether building new church structures or conducting weeklong schools or camps for children and teens, these volunteers help God's work continue to expand and grow. Although the Church of the Nazarene always welcomes more pastors and missionaries to its number, there are many ways to serve God while continuing a personal career.

Nazarenes in local congregations gather for worship and learning, for Bible study and prayer, for children's ministry or youth events. They gather for coffee and fellowship, for knitting and crafting, for choir rehearsal or worship-team practice. Nazarenes believe in getting together to learn, serve, and grow in Christ, becoming more godly, more Christlike, together.

Again, welcome to the Nazarene church family. Our churches come in all sizes. Some have large congregations, but most are small. Yet our congregations—both large and small—are friendly and welcoming. Our doors are open to everyone who wants to join us. We value the love and fellowship that comes from belonging to a family and having a valuable place in that family, and we want to share that love and fellowship with you. We're glad you are considering joining our worldwide Nazarene family! We hope you'll feel welcome here. We're eager to get to know you! May God's light make your pathways brighter (Proverbs 4:18).

APPENDIX

The Holy Spirit is the great Guide in righteous living. Love for Christ is expressed in a desire to do his will. And his will is expressed in the Scriptures. There are times when the church body must stand together on certain social issues. There are times when years of mature experience have produced helpful guidelines concerning a Christlike lifestyle. The Church of the Nazarene deals with social issues and lifestyle questions in the Covenant of Christian Conduct.

The Covenant of Christian Conduct

THE CHRISTIAN LIFE

SANCTITY OF HUMAN LIFE

HUMAN SEXUALITY AND MARRIAGE

CHRISTIAN STEWARDSHIP

CHURCH OFFICERS

RULES OF ORDER

AMENDING THE COVENANT OF CHRISTIAN
CONDUCT

A. The Christian Life

28. The church joyfully proclaims the good news that we may be delivered from all sin to a new life in Christ. By the grace of God we Christians are "to put off the old self"—the old patterns of conduct as well as the old carnal mind—and are "to put on the new self"—a new and holy way of life as well as the mind of Christ.

(Ephesians 4:17–24)

28.1. The Church of the Nazarene purposes to relate timeless biblical principles to contemporary society in such a way that the doctrines and covenants of the church may be known and understood in many lands and within a variety of cultures. We hold that the Ten Commandments, as reaffirmed in the New Testament teachings of Jesus Christ, demonstrated most fully and concisely in the Great Commandment and the Sermon on the Mount constitute the basic Christian ethic.

28.2. It is further recognized that there is validity in the concept of the collective Christian conscience as illuminated and guided by the Holy Spirit. The Church of the Nazarene, as an international expression of the Body of Christ, acknowledges its responsibility to seek ways to particularize the Christian life so as to lead to a holiness ethic. The historic ethical standards of the church are expressed in part in the following items. They should be followed carefully and conscientiously as guides and helps to holy living. Those who violate the conscience of the church do so at their own peril and to the hurt of the witness of the church. Culturally conditioned adaptations shall be referred to and approved by the Board of General Superintendents.

28.3. The Church of the Nazarene believes this new and holy way of life involves practices to be avoided and redemptive acts of love to be accomplished for the souls, minds, and bodies of our neighbors. One redemptive arena of love involves the special relationship Jesus had, and commanded His disciples to have, with the poor of this world; that His Church ought, first, to keep itself simple and free from an emphasis on wealth and extravagance and, second, to give itself to the care, feeding, clothing, and shelter of the poor and marginalized. Throughout the Bible and in the life and example of Jesus, God identifies with and assists the poor, the oppressed, and those in society who cannot speak for themselves. In the same way, we, too, are called to identify with and to enter into solidarity with the poor. We hold that compassionate ministry to the poor includes acts of charity as well as a struggle to provide opportunity, equality, and justice for the poor. We further believe the Christian's responsibility to the poor is an essential aspect of the life of every believer who seeks a faith that works through love. We believe

Christian holiness to be inseparable from ministry to the poor in that it drives the Christian beyond their own individual perfection and toward the creation of a more just and equitable society and world. Holiness, far from distancing believers from the desperate economic needs of people in this world, motivates us to place our means in the service of alleviating such need and to adjust our wants in accordance with the needs of others.

(Exodus 23:11; Deuteronomy 15:7; Psalms 41:1; 82:3; Proverbs 19:17; 21:13; 22:9; Jeremiah 22:16; Matthew 19:21; Luke 12:33; Acts 20:35; 2 Corinthians 9:6; Galatians 2:10)

28.4. In listing practices to be avoided we recognize that no catalog, however inclusive, can hope to encompass all forms of evil throughout the world. Therefore it is imperative that our people earnestly seek the aid of the Spirit in cultivating a sensitivity to evil that transcends the mere letter of the law; remembering the admonition: "Test them all; hold on to what is good, reject every kind of evil."

(1 Thessalonians 5:21–22)

28.5. Our leaders and pastors are expected to give strong emphasis in our periodicals and from our pulpits to such fundamental biblical truths as will develop the faculty of discrimination between the evil and the good.

28.6. Education is of the utmost importance for the social and spiritual well-being of society.

Nazarene educational organizations and institutions, such as Sunday Schools, schools (birth through secondary), child care centers, adult care centers, colleges, and seminaries, are expected to teach children, youth, and adults biblical principles and ethical standards in such a way that our doctrines may be known. This practice may be instead of or in addition to public schools. The education from public sources should be complemented by holiness teaching in the home. Christians should also be encouraged to work in and with public institutions to witness to and influence these institutions for God's kingdom.

(Matthew 5:13–14)

29. We hold specifically that the following practices should be avoided:

29.1. Entertainments that are subversive of the Christian ethic. Our people, both as Christian individuals and in Christian family units, should govern themselves by three principles. One is the Christian stewardship of leisure time. A second principle is the recognition of the Christian obligation to apply the highest moral standards of Christian living. Because we are living in a day of great moral confusion in which we face the potential encroachment of the evils of the day into the sacred precincts of our homes through various avenues such as current literature, radio, television, personal computers, and the Internet, it is essential that the most rigid safeguards be observed to keep our homes from becoming secularized and worldly. However, we hold that entertainment that endorses and encourages holy living, that affirms scriptural values, and that supports the sacredness of the marriage vow and the exclusivity of the marriage covenant, should be affirmed and encouraged. We especially encourage our young people to use their gifts in media and the arts to influence positively this pervasive part of culture. The third principle is the obligation to witness against whatever trivializes or blasphemes God, as well as such social evils as violence, sensuality, pornography, profanity, and the occult, as portrayed by and through the commercial entertainment industry in its many forms and to endeavor to bring about the demise of enterprises known to be the purveyors of this kind of entertainment. This would include the avoidance of all types of entertainment ventures and media productions that produce, promote, or feature the violent, the sensual, the pornographic, the profane, or the occultic, or which feature or glamorize the world's philosophy of secularism, sensualism, and materialism and undermine God's standard of holiness of heart and life.

This necessitates the teaching and preaching of these moral standards of Christian living, and that our people be taught to use prayerful discernment in continually choosing the "high road" of holy living. We therefore call upon our leaders and pastors to give strong emphasis in our periodicals and from our pulpits to such fundamental truths as will develop the principle of discrimination between the evil and good to be found in these media.

We suggest that the standard given to John Wesley by his mother, namely, "whatever weakens your reason, impairs the tenderness of your conscience, obscures your sense of God, or takes off the relish of spiritual things, whatever increases the authority of your body over mind, that thing for you is sin," form the basis for this teaching of discrimination. (28.2–28.4, 926–931)

(Romans 14:7–13; 1 Corinthians 10:31–33; Ephesians 5:1–18; Philippians 4:8–9; 1 Peter 1:13–17; 2 Peter 1:3–11)

29.2. Lotteries and other forms of gambling, whether legal or illegal. The church holds that the final result of these practices is detrimental both to the individual and society.

(Matthew 6:24–34; 2 Thessalonians 3:6–13; 1 Timothy 6:6–11; Hebrews 13:5–6; 1 John 2:15–17)

29.3. Membership in oath-bound secret orders or societies including but not limited to those such as Freemasonry. The quasi-religious nature of such organizations dilutes the Christian's commitment, and their secrecy contravenes the Christian's open witness. This issue will be considered in conjunction with paragraph 112.1 regarding church membership.

(1 Corinthians 1:26-31; 2 Corinthians 6:14-7:1; Ephesians 5:11-16; James 4:4; 1 John 2:15-17)

29.4. All forms of dancing that detract from spiritual growth and break down proper moral inhibitions and reserve.

(Matthew 22:36-39; Romans 12:1-2; 1 Corinthians 10:31-33; Philippians 1:9-11; Colossians 3:1-17)

29.5. The use of intoxicating liquors as a beverage, or trafficking therein; giving influence to, or voting for, the licensing of places for the sale of the same; using illicit drugs or trafficking therein; using of tobacco in any of its forms, or trafficking therein.

In light of the Holy Scriptures and human experience concerning the ruinous consequences of the use of alcohol as a beverage, and in light of the findings of medical science regarding the detrimental effect of both alcohol and tobacco to the body and mind, as a community of faith committed to the pursuit of a holy life, our position and practice is abstinence rather than moderation. Holy Scripture teaches that our body is the temple of the Holy Spirit. With loving regard for ourselves and others, we call our people to total abstinence from all intoxicants.

Furthermore, our Christian social responsibility calls us to use any legitimate and legal means to minimize the availability of both beverage alcohol and tobacco to others. The widespread incidence of alcohol abuse in our world demands that we embody a position that stands as a witness to others. (929–931)

(Proverbs 20:1; 23:29–24:2; Hosea 4:10–11; Habakkuk 2:5; Romans 13:8; 14:15–21; 15:1–2; 1 Corinthians 3:16–17; 6:9–12, 19–20; 10:31–33; Galatians 5:13–14, 21; Ephesians 5:18)

(Only unfermented wine should be used in the sacrament of the Lord's Supper.) (515.4, 532.7, 533.2, 534.1, 700)

29.6. The use of stimulants, depressants, hallucinogens and other intoxicants outside proper medical care and guidance.

In light of medical evidence outlining the dangers of such substances, along with scriptural admonitions to remain in responsible control of mind and body, we choose to abstain from intoxicants, stimulants, depressants, and hallucinogens outside proper medical care and guidance, regardless of the legality and availability of such substances.

(Matthew 22:37–39; 27:34; Romans 12:1–2; 1 Corinthians 6:19–20; 9:24–27)

B. Sanctity of Human Life

30. The Church the Nazarene believes in the sanctity of human life and strives to protect against abortion, embryonic stem cell research, euthanasia, and the withholding of reasonable medical care to handicapped or elderly.

30.1. Induced Abortion. The Church of the Nazarene affirms the sanctity of human life as established by God the Creator and believes that such sanctity extends to the child not yet born. Life is a gift from God. All human life, including life developing in the womb, is created by God in His image and is, therefore, to be nurtured, supported, and protected. From the moment of conception, a child is a human being with all of the developing characteristics of human life, and this life is dependent on the mother for its continued development. Therefore, we believe that human life must be respected and protected from the moment of conception. We oppose induced abortion by any means, when used for either personal convenience or population control. We oppose laws that allow abortion. Realizing that there are rare, but real medical conditions wherein the mother or the unborn child, or both, could not survive the pregnancy, termination of the pregnancy should only be made after sound medical and Christian counseling.

Responsible opposition to abortion requires our commitment to the initiation and support of programs designed to provide care for mothers and children. The crisis of an unwanted pregnancy calls for the community of believers (represented only by those for whom knowledge of the crisis is appropriate) to provide a context of love, prayer, and counsel. In such instances, support can take the form of counseling centers, homes for expectant mothers, and the creation or utilization of Christian adoption services.

The Church of the Nazarene recognizes that consideration of abortion as a means of ending an unwanted pregnancy often occurs because Christian standards of sexual responsibility have been ignored. Therefore the church calls for persons to practice the ethic of the New Testament as it bears upon human sexuality and to deal with the issue of abortion by placing it within the larger framework of biblical principles that provide guidance for moral decision making.

(Genesis 2:7, 9:6; Exodus 20:13; 21:12-16, 22-25; Leviticus 18:21; Job 31:15; Psalms 22:9; 139:3-16; Isaiah 44:2, 24; 49:5; Jeremiah 1:5; Luke 1:15, 23-25, 36-45; Acts 17:25; Romans 12:1-2; 1 Corinthians 6:16; 7:1ff.; 1 Thessalonians 4:3-6)

The Church of the Nazarene also recognizes that many have been affected by the tragedy of abortion. Each local congregation and individual believer is urged to offer the message of forgiveness by God for each person who has experienced abortion. Our local congregations are to be communities of redemption and hope to all who suffer physical, emotional, and spiritual pain as a result of the willful termination of a pregnancy.

(Romans 3:22-24; Galatians 6:1)

30.2. Genetic Engineering and Gene Therapy. The Church of the Nazarene supports the use of genetic engineering to achieve gene therapy. We recognize that gene therapy can lead to preventing and curing disease, and preventing and curing anatomical and mental disorders. We oppose any use of genetic engineering that promotes social injustice, disregards the dignity of persons, or that attempts to achieve racial, intellectual, or social superiority over others (eugenics). We oppose initiation of DNA studies whose results might encourage or support human abortion as an alternative to term live birth. In all cases, humility, a respect for the inviolable dignity of human life, human equality before God, and a commitment to mercy and justice should govern genetic engineering and gene therapy.

30.3. Human Embryonic Stem Cell Research and Other Medical/Scientific Endeavors that Destroy Human Life after Conception. The Church of the Nazarene strongly encourages the scientific community to aggressively pursue advances in stem cell technology obtained from sources such as adult human tissues, placenta, umbilical cord blood, animal sources, and other non-human embryonic sources. This has the righteous end of attempting to bring healing to many, without violating the sanctity of human life. Our stand on human embryonic stem cell research flows from our affirmation that the human embryo is a person made in the image of God. Therefore, we oppose the use of stem cells produced from human embryos for research, therapeutic interventions, or any other purpose.

As future scientific advances make new technologies available, we strongly support this research when it does not violate the sanctity of human life or other moral, biblical laws. However, we oppose the destruction of human embryos for any purpose and any type of research that takes the life of a human after conception. Consistent with this view, we oppose the use, for any purpose, of tissue derived from aborted human fetuses.

30.4. Human Cloning. We oppose the cloning of an individual human being. Humankind is valued by God, who created us in His image, and the cloning of an individual human being treats that being as an object, thus denying the personal dignity and worth bestowed on us by our Creator.

30.5. Euthanasia (Including Physician Assisted Suicide). We believe that euthanasia (intentionally ending the life of a terminally ill person, or one who has a debilitating and incurable disease that is not immediately life-threatening, for the purpose of ending suffering) is incompatible with the Christian faith. This applies when euthanasia is requested or consented to by the terminally ill person (voluntary euthanasia) and when the terminally ill person is not mentally competent to give consent (involuntary euthanasia). We believe that the historic rejection of euthanasia by the Christian church is confirmed by Christian convictions that derive from the Bible and that are central to the Church's confession of faith in Jesus Christ as Lord. Euthanasia violates Christian confidence in God as the sovereign Lord of life by claiming sovereignty for oneself; it violates our role as stewards before God; it contributes to an erosion of the value the Bible places on human life and community; it attaches too much importance to the cessation of suffering; and it reflects a human arrogance before a graciously sovereign God. We urge our people to oppose all efforts to legalize euthanasia.

30.6. Allowing to Die. When human death is imminent, we believe that either withdrawing or not originating artificial life-support systems is permissible within the range of Christian faith and practice. This position applies to persons who are in a persistent vegetative state and to those for whom the application of extraordinary means for prolonging life provide no reasonable hope for a return to health. We believe that when death is imminent, nothing in the Christian faith requires that the process of dying be artificially postponed. As Christians we trust in God's faithfulness and have the hope of eternal life. This makes it possible for Christians to accept death as an expression of faith in Christ who overcame death on our behalf and robbed it of its victory.

C. Human Sexuality and Marriage

31. The Church of the Nazarene views human sexuality as one expression of the holiness and beauty that God the Creator intended. Because all humans are beings created in the image of God, they are of inestimable value and worth. As a result we believe that human sexuality is meant to include more than the sensual experience, and is a gift of God designed to reflect the whole of our physical and relational createdness.

As a holiness people, the Church of the Nazarene affirms that the human body matters to God. Christians are both called and enabled by the transforming and sanctifying work of the Holy Spirit to glorify God in and with our bodies. Our senses, our sexual appetites, our ability to experience pleasure, and our desire for connection to another are shaped out of the very character of God. Our bodies are good, very good.

We affirm belief in a God whose creation is an act of love. Having experienced God as holy love, we understand the Trinity to be a unity of love among Father, Son, and Holy Spirit. Therefore, we are made with a yearning for connection with others at the core of our being. That yearning is ultimately fulfilled as we live in covenanted relationship with God, the creation, and loving one's neighbor as one's self. Our creation as social beings is both good and beautiful. We reflect the image of God in our capacity to relate and our desire to do so. The people of God are formed as one in Christ, a rich community of love and grace.

Within this community, believers are called to live as faithful members of the body of Christ. Singleness among the people of God is to be valued and sustained by the rich fellowship of the church and the communion of the saints. To live as a single person is to engage, as Jesus did, in the intimacy of community, surrounded by friends, welcoming and being welcomed to tables, and expressing faithful witness.

Also within this community, we affirm that some believers are called to be married. As defined in Genesis, "a man leaves his father and mother and is united to his wife, and they become one flesh." (Genesis 2:24) The marriage covenant, a reflection of the covenant between God and the people of God, is one of exclusive sexual fidelity, unselfish service, and social witness. A woman and a man publicly devote themselves to one another as a witness to the way God loves. Marital intimacy is intended to reflect the union of Christ and the Church, a mystery of grace. It is also God's intention that in this sacramental union the man and woman may experience the joy and pleasure of sexual intimacy and from this act of intimate love new life may enter the world and into a covenantal community of care. The Christ-centered home ought to serve as a primary location for spiritual formation. The church is to take great care in the formation of marriage through premarital counseling and teaching that denotes the sacredness of marriage.

The Scriptural story, however, also includes the sad chapter of the fracturing of human desire in the Fall, resulting in behaviors that elevate self-sovereignty, damage and objectify the other, and darken the path of human desire. As fallen beings, we have experienced this evil on every level—personal and corporate. The principalities and powers of a fallen world have saturated us with lies about our sexuality. Our desires have been twisted by sin and we are turned inward on ourselves. We have also contributed to the fracturing of the creation by our willful choice to violate the love of God and live on our own terms apart from God.

Our brokenness in the areas of sexuality takes many forms, some due to our own choosing and some brought into our lives via a broken world. However, God's grace is sufficient in our weaknesses, enough to bring conviction, transformation, and sanctification in our lives. Therefore, in order to resist adding to the brokenness of sin and to be able to witness to the beauty and uniqueness of God's holy purposes for our bodies, we believe members of the body of Christ, enabled by the Spirit, can and should refrain from:

- **Unmarried sexual intercourse and other forms of inappropriate sexual bonding.** Because we believe that it is God's intention for our sexuality to be lived out in the covenantal union between one woman and one man, we believe that these practices often lead to the objectification of the other in a relationship. In all its forms, it also potentially harms our ability to enter into the beauty and holiness of Christian marriage with our whole selves.

- **Sexual activity between people of the same sex.** Because we believe that it is God's intention for our sexuality to be lived out in the covenantal union between one woman and one man, we believe the practice of same-sex sexual intimacy is contrary to God's will for human sexuality. While a person's homosexual or bi-sexual attraction may have complex and differing origins, and the implication of this call to sexual purity is costly, we believe the grace of God is sufficient for such a calling. We recognize the shared responsibility of the body of Christ to be a welcoming, forgiving, and loving community where hospitality, encouragement, transformation, and accountability are available to all.

- **Extra-marital sexual relations.** Because we believe this behavior is a violation of the vows that we made before God and within the body of Christ, adultery is a selfish act, a family-destroying choice, and an offense to the God who has loved us purely and devotedly.
- **Divorce.** Because marriage is intended to be a life-long commitment, the fracturing of the covenant of marriage, whether initiated personally, or by the choice of a spouse, falls short of God's best intentions. The church must take care in preserving the marriage bond where wise and possible, and offering counsel and grace to those wounded by divorce.
- **Practices such as polygamy or polyandry.** Because we believe that the covenantal faithfulness of God is reflected in the monogamous commitment of husband and wife, these practices take away from the unique and exclusive fidelity intended in marriage.

Sexual sin and brokenness is not only personal but pervades the systems and structures of the world. Therefore, as the church bears witness to the reality of the beauty and uniqueness of God's holy purposes we also believe the church should refrain from and advocate against:

- **Pornography in all its forms, which is desire gone awry.** It is the objectification of people for selfish sexual gratification. This habit destroys our capacity to love unselfishly.

- **Sexual violence in any form, including rape, sexual assault, sexual bullying, hateful speech, marital abuse, incest, sex trafficking, forced marriage, female genital mutilation, bestiality, sexual harassment, and the abuse of minors and other vulnerable populations.** All people and systems that perpetrate sexual violence transgress the command to love and to protect our neighbor. The body of Christ should always be a place of justice, protection, and healing for those who are, who have been, and who continue to be affected by sexual violence. A minor is defined as any human being under the age of 18, unless the age of majority is attained later under a state's or country's own domestic legislation.

Therefore we affirm that:

- **Where sin abounds grace abounds all the more.** Although the effects of sin are universal and holistic, the efficacy of grace is also universal and holistic. In Christ, through the Holy Spirit, we are renewed in the image of God. The old is gone and the new comes. Although the forming of our lives as a new creation may be a gradual process, God's healing is effective in dealing with the brokenness of humanity in the areas of sexuality.

- **The human body is the temple of the Holy Spirit.** We affirm the need for our sexuality to be conformed to God's will. Our bodies are not our own but have been bought with a price. Therefore, we are called to glorify God in our bodies through a life of yielded obedience.

- **The people of God are marked by holy love.** We affirm that, above all the virtues, the people of God are to clothe themselves with love. The people of God have always welcomed broken people into our gathering. Such Christian hospitality is neither an excusing of individual disobedience nor a refusal to participate redemptively in discerning the roots of brokenness. Restoring humans to the likeness of Jesus requires confession, forgiveness, formative practices, sanctification, and godly counsel—but most of all, it includes the welcome of love which invites the broken person into the circle of grace known as the church. If we fail to honestly confront sin and brokenness, we have not loved. If we fail to love, we cannot participate in God's healing of brokenness.

As the global church receives and ministers to the people of our world, the faithful outworking of these statements as congregations is complex and must be navigated with care, humility, courage, and discernment.

D. Christian Stewardship

32. Meaning of Stewardship. The Scriptures teach that God is the Owner of all persons and all things. We, therefore, are His stewards of both life and possessions. God's ownership and our stewardship ought to be acknowledged, for we shall be held personally accountable to God for the exercise of our stewardship. God, as a God of system and order in all of His ways, has established a system of giving that acknowledges His ownership over all human resources and relationships. To this end all His children should faithfully tithe and present offerings for the support of the gospel. (140)

(Malachi 3:8–12; Matthew 6:24–34; 25:31–46; Mark 10:17–31; Luke 12:13–24; 19:11–27; John 15:1–17; Romans 12:1–13; 1 Corinthians 9:7–14; 2 Corinthians 8:1–15; 9:6–15; 1 Timothy 6:6–19; Hebrews 7:8; James 1:27; 1 John 3:16–18)

32.1. Storehouse Tithing. Storehouse tithing is a scriptural and practical performance of faithfully and regularly placing the tithe into that church to which the member belongs. Therefore, the financing of the church shall be based on the plan of storehouse tithing, and the local Church of the Nazarene shall be regarded by all of its people as the storehouse. All who are a part of the Church of the Nazarene are urged to contribute faithfully one-tenth of all their increase as a minimum financial obligation to the Lord and freewill offerings in addition as God has prospered them for the support of the whole church, local, district, educational, and general. The tithe, provided to the local Church of the Nazarene, shall be considered a priority over all other giving opportunities which God may lay upon the hearts of His faithful stewards, in support of the whole church.

32.2. Fundraising and Distribution. In the light of the scriptural teaching concerning the giving of tithes and offerings for the support of the gospel, and for the erection of church buildings, no Nazarene church should engage in any method of fundraising that would detract from these principles, hinder the gospel message, sully the name of the church, discriminate against the poor, or misdirect the people's energies from promoting the gospel.

In disbursing to meet the requirements of the local, district, educational, and general programs of the Church of the Nazarene, local churches are urged to adopt and practice a financial apportionment plan, and to pay general, educational, and district apportionments monthly. (130, 153, 154–154.2, 516.13)

32.3. Support of the Ministry. "In the same way, the Lord has commanded that those who preach the gospel should receive their living from the gospel" (1 Corinthians 9:14). The church is obligated to support its ministers, who have been called of God, and who, under the direction of the church, have given themselves wholly to the work of the ministry. We urge therefore that the members of the church voluntarily commit themselves to the task of supporting the ministry by gathering money weekly for this holy business and that the pastor's salary be paid regularly every week. (115.4, 115.6, 129.8)

32.4. Life Income Gifts, Planned and Deferred Giving. It is essential in the exercise of Christian stewardship that careful thought be given as to what shall be done with one's income and possessions over which the Lord makes the Christian a steward during this life. The Church of the Nazarene, recognizing the need for faithful stewardship in this life and the God-given vision to leave a legacy for the future, has established the Church of the Nazarene Foundation to enhance Christian stewardship through planned and deferred giving. Civil laws often do not provide for the distribution of an estate in such a way as to glorify God. Each Christian should give attention to the preparation of a last will and testament in a careful and legal manner, and the Church of the Nazarene through its various ministries of missions, evangelism, education, and benevolences—local, district, educational, and general—is recommended for consideration.

32.5. Shared Responsibility for the Denominational Mission. The government of the Church of the Nazarene is representative. Each local congregation supports the overall mission of the church as defined by the General Assembly and implemented through the leadership of the Board of General Superintendents in world evangelism, education, ministerial support, and district ministries.

The Board of General Superintendents and the General Board are authorized and empowered to develop, revise, and maintain a system for raising the World Evangelism Fund and to establish funding goals and responsibilities for local churches through the assembly districts.

Subject to paragraph 337.1, national boards and/or regional advisory councils are authorized and empowered to establish ministerial retirement savings plans on their region. Reporting of such plans shall be as provided in paragraph 337.2. The provisions of paragraph 32.5 shall not apply to the Board of Pensions and Benefits USA.

National boards and/or regional advisory councils are also authorized and empowered to establish support for the higher education institutions on their region.

Each district is authorized and empowered to establish funding goals and responsibilities for local churches for district ministry support through the District Assembly Finance Committee. (238.1, 317.10, 345, 346.3)

E. Church Officers

33. We direct our local churches to elect as church officers active members of the local church who profess the experience of entire sanctification and whose lives bear public witness to the grace of God that calls us to a holy life; who are in harmony with the doctrines, polity, and practices of the Church of the Nazarene; and who support the local church faithfully in attendance, active service, and with tithes and offerings. Church officers should be fully engaged in "making Christlike disciples in the nations." (113.11, 127, 145–147)

F. Rules of Order

34. Subject to the applicable law, the Articles of Incorporation and the Bylaws of government in the *Manual*, the meetings and proceedings of the members of the Church of the Nazarene, local, district, and general, and the committees of the corporation shall be regulated and controlled according to *Robert's Rules of Order Newly Revised* (latest edition) for parliamentary procedure. (113, 205, 300.3)

G. Amending the Covenant of Christian Conduct

35. The provisions of the Covenant of Christian Conduct may be repealed or amended when concurred in by a two-thirds vote of the members present and voting of a given General Assembly.